GREAT
SCIENTISTS & INVENTORS

Elizabeth Blackwell

by Emily James

Pebble® Plus

CAPSTONE PRESS
a capstone imprint

Pebble Plus is published by Capstone Press,
1710 Roe Crest Drive, North Mankato, Minnesota 56003
www.mycapstone.com

Library of Congress Cataloging-in-Publication Data
Names: James, Emily, 1983– author.
Title: Elizabeth Blackwell / by Emily James.
Description: North Mankato, Minnesota : Capstone Press, [2017] | Series:
Pebble plus. Great scientists and inventors | Audience: Ages 4–8. | Audience: K to grade 3. |
Includes bibliographical references and index.
Identifiers: LCCN 2016023236| ISBN 9781515738824 (library binding) |
ISBN 9781515738886 (pbk.) | ISBN 9781515739067 (ebook (pdf)
Subjects: LCSH: Blackwell, Elizabeth, 1821-1910—Juvenile literature. |
Women physicians—New York (State)—Biography—Juvenile literature. |
Women physicians—England—Biography—Juvenile literature. |
Physicians—New York (State)—Biography—Juvenile literature.
Classification: LCC R154.B623 J36 2017 | DDC 610.92 [B] —dc23
LC record available at https://lccn.loc.gov/2016023236

Editorial Credits
Jaclyn Jaycox and Michelle Hasselius, editors; Jennifer Bergstrom, designer;
Jo Miller, media researcher; Steve Walker, production specialist

Photo Credits
Alamy: Mary Evans Picture Library, 7; AP Images, 15, 21; Bridgeman Images: Schlesinger
Library, Radcliffe Institute, Harvard University, 11; Getty Images: Archive Photos/Museum
of the City of New York, 5, Bettmann, cover, 1, 9, 17; Granger, NYC - All rights reserved., 13;
Newscom: Everett Collection, 19

Design Elements: Shutterstock: aliraspberry, Charts and BG, mangpor2004, Ron and Joe,
sumkinn, Yurii Andreichyn

Note to Parents and Teachers

The Great Scientists and Inventors set supports national curriculum standards for
social studies related to people, places, and culture. This book describes and illustrates
the life of Elizabeth Blackwell. The images support early readers in understanding
the text. The repetition of words and phrases helps early readers learn new words.
This book also introduces early readers to subject-specific vocabulary words, which
are defined in the Glossary section. Early readers may need assistance to read some
words and to use the Table of Contents, Glossary, Read More, Internet Sites, Critical
Thinking Using the Common Core, and Index sections of the book.

Printed and bound in China.

PO7886LEOS17

Table of Contents

EARLY LIFE

Elizabeth Blackwell was
born in England on
February 3, 1821. She had
eight brothers and sisters.

Elizabeth in 1850

Elizabeth's parents thought
education was important.
They hired a tutor to teach
their children at home.
Elizabeth studied hard.

a drawing of a tutor with her students

7

In 1832 the Blackwell family moved to New York. After a few years, they moved to Ohio. Elizabeth worked as a teacher after her father died in 1838.

a classroom in 1886

FIRST WOMAN DOCTOR

When Elizabeth was 24, a sick
friend told her she wished there
were female doctors. At the
time, there were none. Elizabeth
knew she could be the first.

Elizabeth had trouble finding a medical school. Most of them did not allow female students. Finally she was accepted to a medical school in New York.

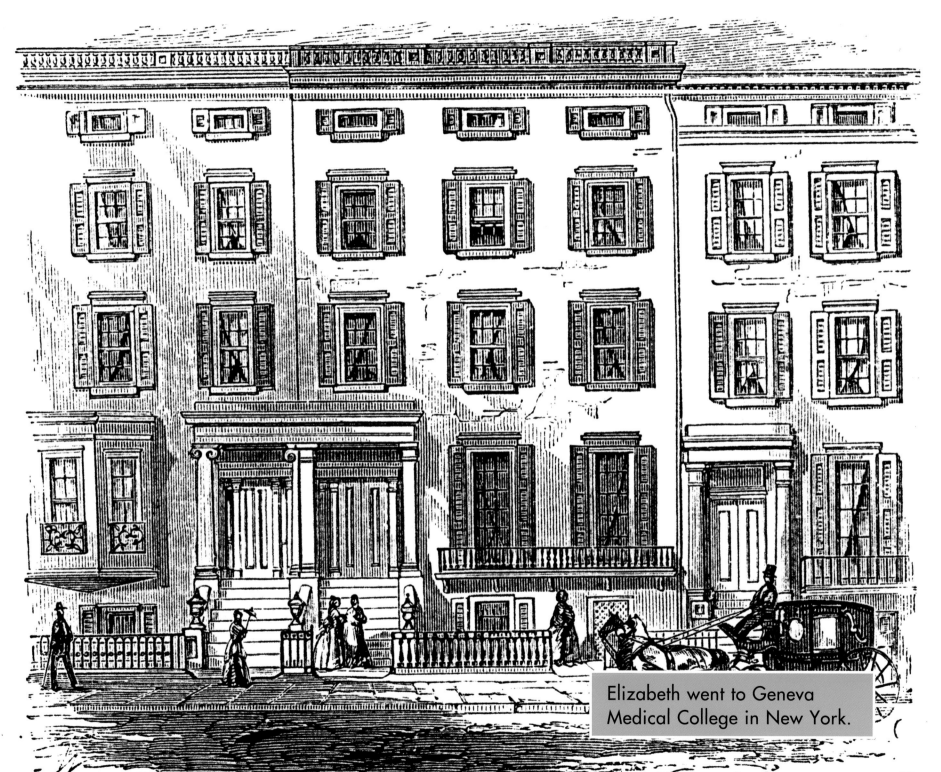

Elizabeth went to Geneva Medical College in New York.

Elizabeth graduated in 1849.

She became the first female doctor

in the United States.

Still most hospitals would not hire

her because she was a woman.

DIPLOMA OF
ELIZABETH BLACKWELL, M.D.
Born at Bristol 3rd February, 1821   Died at Hastings, 31st May, 1910.

Elizabeth's diploma

EARLY WORK

In 1853 Elizabeth opened

her own clinic in New York.

She taught her patients

to eat well, exercise, and

keep clean.

Elizabeth in 1900

MAKING A DIFFERENCE

Elizabeth moved to England

in 1869. She helped open the

first medical school for women.

She inspired many other

women to become doctors.

Female medical students learned about the human body at the Medicine College for Women.

Elizabeth died in 1910.

By then there were more than

7,000 female doctors in the

United States. Elizabeth proved

that a woman can do any job.

21

Glossary

education—the process of teaching and learning

female—woman

graduate—to finish all the required classes at a school

hire—to agree to pay someone to do work for you

hospital—a building where doctors and others work to help people who are very sick or badly hurt

inspire—to influence or encourage other people in a really good way; if someone tells you that you inspire them, you should feel really proud

medical school—a college where people study to become doctors

patient—a person who receives medical care

tutor—a teacher who gives lessons to only one student or a small group of students

Read More

Esbaum, Jill. *Little Kids First Big Book of Who.* Little Kids First Big Book. Washington, D.C.: National Geographic Society, 2015.

Ready, Dee. *Doctors Help.* Our Community Helpers. North Mankato, Minn.: Capstone Press, 2013.

Stone, Tanya Lee. *Who Says Women Can't Be Doctors?: The Story of Elizabeth Blackwell.* New York: Henry Holt and Co., 2013.

Internet Sites

FactHound offers a safe, fun way to find Internet sites related to this book. All of the sites on FactHound have been researched by our staff.

Here's all you do:

Visit *www.facthound.com*

Type in this code: 9781515738824

Super-cool stuff!

Check out projects, games and lots more at
www.capstonekids.com

Critical Thinking Using the Common Core

1. Name three things Elizabeth taught her patients at her clinic in New York. (Key Ideas and Details)

2. Elizabeth opened a medical school in England in 1869. What was important about this school? (Key Ideas and Details)

3. Elizabeth inspired other women to become doctors. What does "inspire" mean? (Craft and Structure)

Index